MAGIC IN PRAGUE

NCQ TITLES

Legal Fictions   Time Pieces
Politics & Letters   Critical Paranoia
On Yeats: Upon a House   On Joyce: 3 easy essays
Drama & Democracy   On Eliot
Locating Theology   Literary Conversions

Film-texts

A Trip to Rome   A Week in Venice
A Short Break in Budapest   Four Days in Athens
Magic in Prague   The Last Priest of Horus
WWW: the weekend that warped the world

Play texts

Darwin: an evolutionary entertainment
Strange Meetings & Shorts

Eliotics

In preparation

Rubbishing Hockney & other reviews
On Collecting Walter Benjamin
Autobiography & Class Consciousness
Considering Canterbury Cathedral

*Though each can be read independently,
these NCQ publications, taken together,
comprise a single hyper-text collection.*

MAGIC IN PRAGUE

a film-text

Bernard Sharratt

New Crisis Quarterly
2015

NEW CRISIS QUARTERLY

ncq@newcrisisquarterly.myzen.co.uk

First published 2015

ISBN : 978-1-910956-16-8

For
Karen & Alex
(with apologies
for the Czech)

This film-text is not written with actual film production in mind. Though it plays with a variety of film genres, it is primarily intended to be read—and imagined.

Prague is an appropriate place as the setting for my characters and my themes, and the script is designed to be easily supplemented by on-line images and maps of the specified sites and scenes. Other film-texts in this 'city' series are set in Athens, Budapest, Rome, and Venice, and the series will probably concludes with *A Last Sight of Europe*.

A film-text is a particularly suitable form for the New Crisis Quarterly imprint, since that name revives the title of an extremely short-lived periodical whose first, only, and final issue appeared in 1984, under the guise of my *The Literary Labyrinth*. Its editorial programme was to publish reviews of imagined books I didn't feel I had the time actually to write, so its readers were cheerfully invited, if so inclined, to write those works themselves. In the same spirit, reading a film-text means that most of the work of imagining the film can be done by you, which is part of the fun of writing them.

B.S.
May Day
2015

FADE IN [PRE-CREDITS:]

1. INT. CONSULTING ROOM.

*Tom Brady, aged late sixties, is seated in the consulting room of a
doctor, Jim, about the same age. They are old friends as well as doctor-
patient. Setting is the University Medical Centre of an English
provincial university campus.*

                    JIM
          So, do you want a cup of tea, Tom?
          I've got nothing stronger here, I'm afraid.
          Even for you.

                    TOM
          Thanks, Jim. No.
          *(He gets up and goes across the room
          to look at an MRI brain scan on a screen.)*
          Funny way to get a death sentence.
          Glad they let *you* tell me. Again, Jim : how long?
          I didn't really take it in first time.
          No bullshit.

                    JIM
          OK, no bullshit. But it's not certain yet
          what *kind* of tumour. Worst case, since you insist,
          maybe six months, or less. If it's *glioblastoma
          multiforme*, next worst but most common,
          around eighteen months, if treatment works.
          But, long shot, you might have up to sixteen years—
          the highest survival record for low grade
          oligodendroglioms—as we cheerfully call 'em.
          But it'll take a biopsy to be absolutely sure.
          Histological examination of tumor tissue samples.
          Standard next step. I can push for that to happen
          as soon as possible. I can even try for next week,
          if we're lucky.

TOM

Lucky? *(pause)* It's bad timing, Jim.
Completely scuppered my retirement plans, eh.
And next week—no chance—not even for this.
I'm doing my swan song—decided I was
performing at my very last conference, ever.
(ironic snort) Beware of what you wish for.
But it's the third time I've agreed to do something
for this lot, and the previous two occasions I had to
pull out at the last minute. I really feel I can't break
this commitment, again. Maybe fate is telling me
otherwise. But I'm going. And I'm train-hopping
across Europe, so won't be back for a week. OK?

JIM

It will have to do. It does give me more time to set
up a full medical case-team. Where are you off to?

TOM

Prague. European Renaissance Association
conference. They meet in a different place each
year. And Prague this year was one of the reasons
for saying yes, again. Haven't been back for years.
Was looking forward to it. I suppose it'll all look a
bit different now. *(rueful pause)* Bugger it. *(pause)*
Well, at least I have a few old friends to meet up
with, for the last time, I suppose. And a favourite
ex-student I haven't seen for a long while.
The department secretary has all the details,
hotel and the rest, and you have my email address.
Let me know what's happening—it's *my* brain
tumour, after all. Do I get a copy of that thing
(the MRI scan). Makes me look like Darth Vader.

JIM

I'll email you one. But don't put it up on the wall,
Tom. Frightens the kiddies.

                    TOM
Remember I don't have any. For a bachelor like me,
keeping in touch with old friends and students is the
nearest I get to family. And especially good friends
like you.

                    JIM
Have a hug, Tom. And then go and have a stiff
drink. Or several.

                    TOM
I see—alcohol can't do any more damage now, eh?
Maybe I should take up smoking again.

(They share a bear hug)

[CREDITS OVER:]

2. EXTERIOR. RAPID SEQUENCE.

Train arriving in the long sweep into main Prague station.
Tom arrives. He makes his way with wheeled luggage through the
arrival concourse, down to the under-area, following signs for taxis.
The kerbside space has a line of taxis and is crowded with haggling
tourists. He joins the queue.

[END CREDITS]

3. PRAGUE STATION. TAXI RANK.

Tom gets to the kerb and asks a taxi driver in English and then in
bad Czech:

                    TOM
How much to 'Hotel at the House of the Golden
Goose '? Er, jak moc 'Hotelu u domu Zlatá Husa'?

TAXI DRIVER
Twelve hundred koruna.
TOM
You're joking! Should be about a hundred —
maximum! Ne, ne.

Taxi driver shrugs. Tom tries another taxi driver.

TOM
Hotelu u domu Zlatá Husa?

TAXI DRIVER 2
One hundred fifty. Euros.

TOM
Euros! Thirty—

TAXI DRIVER 2
Žádném . No deal.

*Tom's wheeled luggage case falls over. As he bends down to pick it up,
he is skilfully pickpocketted, losing his wallet and phone to a well
practised teenage pickpocketer. Tom doesn't notice.
The youngster retreats to the back wall of the area and calmly lights a
cigarette, waiting for more easy pickings, but staying near to the exit
corridor in case.*

*Don McKenzie, aged late-thirties, nondescript, is lounging casually
against a side wall with a cigarette and newspaper.
He sees the pickpocketting, but doesn't intervene.*

*Maria comes from within the station. Maria is about 75, small, feisty,
expensively dressed, confident. She has two large suitcases on wheels.
Goes towards the kerbside and stands near Tom.*

Don is watching her covertly.

Tom tries another taxi driver.

                    TOM
Hotelu u domu Zlatá Husa?

                    TAXI DRIVER 3
Six hundred.

                    TOM *(resigned)*
Four hundred. Koruna.

                    TAXI DRIVER 3
Deal . Šest sto.   Předem .

                    TOM
Předem?

                    TAXI DRIVER 3
In advance.

Tom is about to pay, when he realises his wallet has gone.

                    TOM
Bugger! My wallet!

Realises Maria has heard him swear.

                    TOM
Sorry, Madam. Excuse my language.

                    MARIA
No offence. Can I help?

                    TOM
I've lost my wallet. Now I can't pay for the taxi.

                    MARIA
Lost? You've probably been pickpocketted.
Has anything else gone?

Tom pats his pockets.

TOM

Yes, my phone. Damn. But *(relief)* not my passport.
(hesitates) My wallet has my credit cards and my
Czeck money. My spare wallet only has English
money. Could I possibly ask you to change some
sterling for me so I can take the taxi?

In the background, Don is watching but can't hear their exchange.

MARIA *(joking)*

I'd probably be committing some horrible crime—
unofficial currency exchange—used to be very
inadvisable—and I might give you an exorbitant
exchange rate! But don't worry, the taxi will take
English, American, Euros, Rumanian, Martian
currencies—anything these days—but at an even
worse rate for you. So, I can probably do better
than that—I can perhaps offer you a lift?
My driver is picking me up here.
Where do you need to get to?

TOM

That's very kind of you. My hotel is on the other
side of the river, Hotel Golden Goose

MARIA

I know it. It's almost on my way. No trouble at all.
You are visiting Prague on business?

TOM

Well, yes, I suppose so. Though my business is
actually academic. I teach literature. Tom Brady,
Professor Tom Brady *(offers a handshake)*.
I'm attending a conference here for a few days..

MARIA

On?

TOM

On 'Renaissance drama : Magic and Money'.

MARIA

That sounds most interesting.
You said 'Tom Brady', yes?
But you're in literature, yes? Not—?
I must be thinking of a different Tom Brady.
And I'm Maria. Just call me Maria.

TOM

Your English, if I may say so, is excellent.

MARIA

It should be. I'm English.
It's Czech I still have difficulty with.

A very expensive limousine pulls over. Chauffeur gets out.

MARIA

Ah, the car. Jacub, would you help this gentlemen
with his luggage. We are giving him a lift.

Chauffeur packs Tom's bag into the boot and they get into the car.

*Meanwhile, Don walks casually over to the pickpocket, who spots him
just too late to flee, as Don grips his arm tightly.*

DON
(flourishes an ID card briefly and speaks in rapid Czeck:)
Detektiv Zaman. Předat, že peněženku.
Pokud si nepřejete být zatčen.
[Hand the wallet over. Unless you want to be
arrested.]

PICKPOCKET
Zkurvysyn [You shit].
He hands over Tom's wallet.

DON
A telefon. Pak vypadnout!
[And the phone. Then, vamoose.]

The pickpocket scowls at Don but hands over the phone,
then walks angrily away.

Don makes no attempt to return the wallet or phone to Tom
and pockets them himself. Then he watches Maria's car leave.

In the crowd, Rudy is casually watching all this.
Rudy is thirty-ish, well built and well dressed.
He is amused at Don's encounter with the pickpocket.

Viktor arrives brisky from within the station, with an escort, Joe.
Viktor is about fifty, well-fed and expensively dressed.
Joe is obviously a bodyguard. Joe is pulling two wheeled cases.

Don sees Viktor and clearly recognises him.
Rudy notices the recognition and half-moves towards him.
Don sees this move and promptly turns and disappears into the crowd
and exits the area.

VIKTOR *(in Czech, with subtitles)*
Kdo byl ten muž? [Who was that man?]

RUDY
Možná, že policie. Ale on není normální policajt.
Neviděl jsem ho neviděl. Pravděpodobně o podvod.
[Maybe the police. But he is not a normal cop.
I've not seen him before. Probably a scam.]

VIKTOR
No, jasně že mě zná. Pak utekl. Nelíbí se mi to.
Dostanete auto. Joe, jít za ním.
[Well, he clearly knew who I am. Then scarpered.
I don't like that. You get the car. Joe, go and check
him out.]

Joe follows Don who sees him coming and rapidly leaves the station.

4. IN MARIA'S CAR. DRIVING AWAY FROM THE
STATION

*Tom is just making conversation, but obviously finds Maria
sympathetic .*

> TOM
> Well, the conference is on European renaissance
> drama, various plays about money or magic or both.
> Czech drama really began with a comedy about
> Dives and Lazarus. But most of the relevant plays
> are actually English, *The Alchemist, Volpone, Merchant
> of Venice, Faust , Timon of Athens*—so I get to give the
> main lecture. Probably be my last!

> MARIA
> I'm sure it won't be as bad as all that!

> TOM
> I hope not—though that wasn't quite what I meant.
> *(hesitates)* I haven't been here since the '80s .
> Those Days of Hope. And this will be my last visit.

> MARIA
> Surely you can always come back to Prague?.

> TOM
> *(hesitates)* Sadly, not so. One of those things.
> *(shrugs it off and changes the subject)* But yourself?—
> You're English, but you live in Prague? yes?

> MARIA
> My husband and I moved here after '89.
> He was Czech, but had been in exile ever since the
> '68 Spring. He died four years ago. Sadly.
> But I'm a relatively merry widow. I have my little
> charities and so forth to keep me busy.

The car is stopped in traffic, just by the Dancing House

TOM

Good Lord, that's new.

MARIA

Yes, indeed, Tancici Dum, the Dancing House.
You don't know the story? Comic in its way.
February 1945. Sixty American bombers thought
they were flying over Dresden. Quite a mistake to
make! This whole corner was badly bombed.
Flattened. And right next door lived the Havel
family. Who survived, including the nine-year-old
Vaclav. When he became President he took a
personal interest in making this corner memorable
—it's supposed to symbolise the change from rigid
totalitarianism to a dynamic future. Dancing house.

TOM

Looks more like a crushed tin can!

MARIA

Well, had the young Vaclav Havel been crushed in
that air-raid, perhaps history would have been
different. Chance, accident, destiny, fate—
who knows? Certainly the Dancing House would
never have been built.

They take the bridge across the river and turn right along Zborovska.

5. EXT. OUTSIDE A HOTEL.
[Hotel Julian, Elisky Peskove 11]

Tom gets out of the car and Jacub helps with his luggage.

TOM

That was most kind of you.

MARIA

Not at all. I hope your conference goes well.

He enters the hotel. Car drives away.

6. INT. HOTEL LOBBY DESK.

> TOM
> Tom Brady, Professor Brady. I'm a delegate at the
> Renaissance conference. I need to check in, but
> first can I make an urgent call—to my credit card
> company. My wallet got lifted at the station.

> CLERK
> Professor Brady? Yes, your rooom is booked,
> and *(he checks carefully)* paid for in advance.
> By credit card. I sincerely hope there is no major
> problem. You may use this phone, of course.
> And there is also a phone message for you.

7. INT. CHEAP HOTEL ROOM.

*Don is at his laptop. He is checking out Tom Brady on the net,
and cross-checking names from the list of contacts on Tom's phone.*

8. INT. LOBBY OF THE NATIONAL THEATRE.
EVENING.

*There is a large reception for the many conference delegates.
Various delegates milling around. Tom greets several as old friends.
Various nationalities.*

> TOM
> Ziggi, hello. —Eva, long time. —Çevat, very good
> to see you. —Stefan! —Péter, Agnès. —Tomas.

9. INT. LUXURIOUS LOUNGE OF MARIA'S HOUSE.

Maria is speaking on a phone:

> MARIA
> Yes, I met a colleague of yours today: Tom Brady.
> Do you know him well? *(pause)* Something he said.
> I've got a hunch he thinks he's dying. *(pause)* Yes.

So do you think he might be suitable to join our
little group? *(pause))* Perhaps you might bring him
along tomorrow evening? *(pause)* That's fine.

10. INT. INSIDE THEATRE AUDITORIUM.

A performance is in progress—in Czech—of Pavel Kyrmezer's
Komedie česká o bohatci a Lazarovi—*a biblical play about
Dives and Lazarus, from 1566, played as a riotous comedy.*

11. INT. HOTEL BREAKFAST ROOM.
NEXT MORNING.

*Tom is eating alone at a breakfast table.
Stefan Mazur comes and joins him. Stefan is Polish, elderly.
His English is accented but excellent.*

       STEFAN
Morning Tom. May I join you? *(sits)*
I believe you met an old friend of mine yesterday.
She gave you a lift from the station. Maria Kolar.

       TOM
The Maria Kolar? *(impressed)* So that's who she was.
Wish I'd caught the name.

       STEFAN
Well, you can meet her again if you like.
She rang to invite you to join me for a little
gathering at her place this evening. Should be more
fun than *Volpone* in Czech. She has a huge house up
near the Castle. About 8 o'clock, if you're free.
We can meet here, take a taxi up the hill together.

       TOM
Indeed, yes, Stefan, Be delighted. Maria Kolar, eh.
She did some really good pioneering stuff back in
the 90s. Didn't even know she was still around.

She seemed to have dropped out of the limelight.
Yes, indeed, it'll be a nice way to finish the day—
I'm giving myself a complete day off.

                STEFAN
What you English call 'skyving', is that the word?

                TOM
More or less. I'm having lunch with an old student,
and I'm spending the morning being a tourist,
so I'm skipping most of the programme today.
And I still have to finish writing my paper.
Not that I have anything to say. Rather dreading it.

                STEFAN
You're on tomorrow? You're an old hand.
It won't be a problem.

                TOM
Maybe, but my heart isn't in it. All seems a bit
trivial at the moment. *(pause)*
Stefan, a rather personal question, if I may. *(pause)*
I remember you had that cancer scare a while back.
You were given just six months, yes?
But you came through.

                STEFAN
Well, I'm still here. Is there anything wrong, Tom?

                TOM
I need a spot of practical advice, I think.

12. INT. CHEAP HOTEL ROOM. MORNING.

Don speaks on mobile phone:

                DON
Yes, it's coming together nicely. Maria got back
from her monthly visit to Basel yesterday.

And my Basel source is playing ball. He thinks he's
going to lose his job soon anyway, so is happy to
spill a few beans. For a consideration, of course.
The meeting is presumably tonight. I'll check it out.
(pause, listens) Well, it won't give me any major leads
I don't already have—though there seems to be one
new face, at least, a Tom Brady. I've not seen him
before. *(pause)* Yes, from England, here under
cover of some academic conference. He's got a
couple of Prague contacts not on Maria's own list,
and he has a very different network in England.
Quite a few City people—so they may be branching
out. *(pause)* No, I did *not* hack his phone. Well, not
quite. Just don't ask. *(As he speaks he checks for new
messages on Tom's phone and then puts it down on his table.)*
Oh, one other thing. Might be just coincidence,
but I spotted an old acquaintance yesterday.
Viktor Černy is in town. *(pause)* Yes. But for what?
Presumably he's still working with the Yukov group.
Any rate, his goons spotted me. Lemonade Joe even
followed me. It's OK—I lost him. *(pause)*
Well, it's not my territory any more, of course.
(pause) Unless, yes, just maybe, there's a connection.
Now, that *would* be interesting. What if they got off
the same train? I'll chase my Basel contact again this
evening. *(pause).* Yes, I'll pass on anything I get —
if I can't use it myself! *(laughs)* OK, that's it for now.
I'm going to spend the day at some local art
galleries. Apparently they're good places for doing
one's laundry. Check in tomorrow.

13. EXT. PRAGUE CENTRAL AREA.
LEISURELY SEQUENCE.

Brief shots and fades:

Tom strolls the main tourist sights, clearly melancholy and preoccupied.

*He stops in front of the astronomical clock—and grimaces ruefully at
the passing of time. He doesn't wait for the chimes.*

In the Kafka Bookshop, he picks up a few books, then thinks to himself, and puts them back.

In the Old Synagogue Cemetery, he looks at graves piled on top of each other. Shudders.

Tom walks across the crowded Charles Bridge to Old Town, weaving between tourists and fending off painters and caricaturists.

In the cathedral, he looks disdainfully at the elaborately gilded statue of Saint Nepomuk.

In the Castle courtyard, he turns a corner into Alchemists Lane, takes one look at the queue and milling crowds and turns away.

Tom checks his watch and quickly walks out of the castle forecourt and down the hill.

14. INT. SHOP.
[The Eclectic Gallery, at the corner of Jánský Vršek]

ROISIN & ANDRIY. Both in their forties. Roisin is Irish, Andriy is Ukrainian. The shop is elegant and expensive, mainly art works and jewellery, textile handbags and printed scarves, with various Tarot card sets prominently on display.

Tom enters.

> ROISIN
> Tom, it's good to see you again. Welcome!
> *(warm embrace)* You've not met Andriy.
> Tom, Andriy. Andriy, Tom.

> ANDRIY
> Good to meet you, Tom. Finally. Roisin's told me
> about you. You were her supervisor, yes?

TOM
Hello Andriy. A very long time ago. *(smiles)*
'Narrative theory and multi-layer fictions.'
James Joyce and all that. Not much call for literary
theory, these days!

ROISIN
Well, it's what got me into hypertext, Tom.
Pretty advanced for its day! That's how I teamed up
with Andriy, doing all that early Web stuff..

TOM
You were a web designer, Andriy, or a programmer?

ANDRIY
Programmer, sort of. *(hesitates)* I was in a Soviet
military hacking outfit before it all collapsed in '89.
But what I'd always wanted to do was graphic
design. That was my original training.

ROISIN *(smiles at Andriy)*
So, with a bit of post-Soviet persuasion, he put his
design skills into a rampant capitalist enterprise.

TOM
Yes, I remember—your start-up companies did
pretty well for themselves— 'Entangled Web', in
London, and then 'Pursued by a Bear' when you
moved to Prague. Not a great name, mind!—
but you were damn successful.

ROISIN
Till the dot.com bubble wiped out half our clients,
of course.

ANDRIY
Roisin tells me you'd worked in computing yourself,
back in the 80s,

                TOM
Well, it was great fun in those days. Lots of new
developments, exciting times. Riding the wave. But
then it all went utterly and boringly commercial.
By the mid-90s, all my computing students wanted
was to make a million quid by next week. After the
dot com bubble burst, most ended up in the City.
So I hightailed it back to teaching literature.—

                ROISIN
—and Andriy and I went back to good old-
fashioned graphic design. Doing ad-led websites
had become like making films mainly for the
product placements. So we sold up the business --

                TOM
—And now you've got this shop. *(looks around)*
Some nice stuff. Designer handbags. Lovely
scarves. And lots of Tarot cards!
(He picks up some of the Tarot sets) The Bohemian
Tarot Set. The Prague Tarot. I looked at your
website. And this is your main product line, yes?
(smiles) Well, so long as you don't actually believe in
all this Tarot business!

                ROISIN
Now, don't scoff, Tom. I remember that tone.
(smiles) And you're to blame anyway, you know.
It was partly another spin-off from that thesis.
Remember I worked on Calvino's *Castle of Crossed
Destinies*—that got me interested in Tarot—Then
The Saragossa Manuscript—magic and the occult!
And Kafka hooked me on Prague. It's all your fault!

                ANDRIY *(handling some of the work)*
We like beautiful objects, Tom, and we make
deliberately limited editions of some of these
packs—so they sell, they have scarcity value,
become collectors items.

ROISIN *(amused)*
You're not convinced, are you, Tom. You still think
people should only make something socially useful.
I agree —if we can find it. And we think we have.
                TOM *(puts his hands up in mock surrender)*
I'm off-duty. I'm only here for the lunch!

                ROISIN
Ah, lunch, yes. We should be on our way.
OK, we're eating up the hill. Fantastic view. Let me
lock up the shop and we can walk up to Bella Vista.

15. INT. A SMALL ART GALLERY.

*Don is idly looking at a whole wall of very mediocre paintings of
picturesque Prague. Not impressed..*

                DON *(selects one)*
How much?

                GALLERY OWNER
Five hundred euros. For cash.

                DON
No way. How many do you sell at that price?

                GALLERY OWNER
(shrugs indifferently)

16. EXT. STREET OUTSIDE THE ART GALLERY.

Joe is watching.

17. EXT. TERRACE RESTAURANT AT BELLA VISTA,
OVERLOOKING THE CITY.

*Tom, Roisin and Andriy are seated at a table with a splendid view
over the city.They are nearlyy through a good meal*

TOM *(He is in full flow, after a drink or two—)*
So, yes, Andriy, I was here very briefly in '68, as a
student, and then came back a few times later to
Charter '77 seminars. Both periods seemed hopeful.
At the time. But I'm afraid I don't really see what's
happened since '89 as hopeful. Rather the reverse.
Yes, the Czechs and everybody else threw off a
deadening Soviet model, the repressive imperialism
of it all, and so on, and so on—But it wasn't really a
'revolution', was it, velvet or otherwise, just a sort of
historical regression. Back to those old old models,
nationalism and capitalism. Perhaps combined,
as good old fashioned Fascism once again.
Who knows? Communism, or just actually existing
socialism, with all its failures and corruptions, its
idiocies and cruelties, was at least a promise of *some*
kind of *alternative* to greedy corporate profits and
mindless individual consumerism. It held out just a
glimpse of the *option* of a systemic alternative to
capitalist exploitation of the entire globe. And after
that crap Soviet model crashed, what did you end
up with in Russia—seven oligarchs controlling half
the country—

ROISIN *(interrupts the flow)*
You haven't changed, Tom. But the world has.
It's no longer communism versus old fashioned
capitalism. You can't still be loyal to marxism,
surely?

TOM
Yes, I damn well can. I still think the basic analysis
is right. And the basic values are right. Look, if
Lenin could explain why capitalism stinks starting
from a glass of water, let me try it with just a glass
of Pilsner. *(He picks up his beer glass)* One of the first
things the Czechoslovak government did after 1989
was the State Companies Act—just like Russia
under Yeltsin, all state-owned businesses were

handed over to ex-bureaucrats who could do what they wanted with them. Anyone who could quote Hayek or Milton Friedman and could speak American was suddenly an expert entrepreneur. But those people were only interested in stripping what had been public assets. And one of the biggest so-called 'privatisations' here was the Investment and Postal Bank. Remember that? It was the third largest bank in the country, with three million customers, and a lot of clout. In 1998 the last state shares in it were finally sold off. To Nomura, the big Japanese bank. Within three years, IPB's Board of Directors were under arrest for siphoning off *fifty-seven billion* koruna through loan fraud, insider trading, and property scams. *And* covering it all up with manipulated audits and financial misreporting. The bank's bad loans were actually about *five billion dollars*—that was a third of the Czech government's overall budget at the time! When IPB was finally sold on to a Belgian bank—for just one koruna!— it was the Czech state, the Czech people, who were left with those five billion dollars in bad loans. And in the meanwhile, Nomura had sold off IPB's stake in Czech breweries, including the wonderful Pilsner. *(He raises his glass in a mock salutation).* Nomura bought them for about 250 million dollars, pooled them with other Czech beer assets, and then sold the lot to South African Breweries —for a whopping six hundred million dollars. Hundred per cent profit. That deal ' lost ' IPB itself about 170 million dollars. But Nomura made a huge profit— and then walked away. So, every time you drink a glass of good old Pilsner beer, think of what happened to those once-public assets—and for whose benefit? Here's to capitalism! *(He takes a drink in ironic toast)*

ROISIN

That's not capitalism, Tom. That's just crime.
And it certainly doesn't make marxism a better
alternative—

TOM

But Marxism *isn't* an 'alternative' to capitalism. It's
an alternative way of *analysing* what capitalism is,
how it works, and fails to work. It's an *alternative
analysis* to the standard cretinous orthodoxy of neo-
liberal economic theory and ideology. A marxist
analysis only helps show us what an alternative
would have to involve. But Marx himself had very
little to say about what 'communism' would be in
practice—he didn't offer blueprints for the future—
that would be like trying to predict in the 12th
century how today's global economy was going to
be organised! Marx was a historian not a crystal ball
gazer—he thought capitalism had some basic
contradictions and he showed why it's in permanent
crisis—why it's always in a crisis for most people
under its control. How the people who make the
food on this table are exploited, are systematically
not paid as much as the value of what they produce
—otherwise there would be no surplus value for the
capitalist to expropriate, no profit for his capital
investment to bring back a return for him —

ROISIN *(cuts him off)*

— And no meal for you to enjoy today, Tom!
Look, you'd probably say that I'm now a capitalist—
I put the money from the sale of the web company
into the shop, into the business. Yes, that was
'capital'. But we also do the work ourselves, we
design the products, we sell them. Like most
businesses, we're small-scale, innovative, and make a
small profit. I'm creating things, and a bit of wealth
along the way. How am I 'exploiting' anybody?

TOM

Where do you get the raw materials from, Roisin,
the leather in those handbags, the cotton in those
scarves? Where is the printing for the Tarot cards
done? Who actually *makes* the things.

ROISIN

OK, we out-source some of the work, yes, but we
pay a good wage. And it's *our* input, not theirs that
gives our products extra value. The handbags
wouldn't sell for nearly as much if they weren't
made according to our designs. This notion that it's
only somehow the 'worker', the guy who physically
makes an object, that gives it value is complete
nonsense. The profit, the surplus, comes from *all*
the inputs working together. Including a capitalist
who only invests money in the business. Look at
this restaurant—where do you draw the line
between 'worker' and so-called capitalist?—is the
cook the exploiter of the farmer who grew the
vegetables?—is the waiter somehow defrauding the
customers just by waiting on them?—you're paying
for good cooking and a great view. That's surely
extra 'value ' —or we could have had a bag of crisps
sitting in the shop!

ANDRIY *(to passing waiter)*

Na účet, prosím.

TOM

Alright, I partly agree. At that level, the restaurant
could simply be a cooperative—making things
involves several kinds of input. And several kinds of
surplus—if the cook is any good, the meal will taste
much better. So the surplus, the profit, could be
shared according to the input—*from* each according
to his or her *ability*. But communism is also about:
to each according to her or his *needs*. And the
capitalist form of economic organisation as such has

no way of ensuring that—since those needs may not yield a profit. The only needs *thinkable* within a capitalist economy are the needs expressed in market terms, as commodities to be paid for. To be bought and sold. But work isn't bought at the price of the value it produces. So, in order to provide for people's needs, even their most basic needs, you have to have state-provided welfare—but now capitalism is trying to turn even those basic needs themselves into saleable commodites, as energy, water, transport, education, health, shelter, even the police, all get completely privatised, turned into profitable investments. But then they're re-organised to generate a profit, not in order to meet people's needs. So if there's not 'enough' profit, those needs are simply not met. People starve, have no water, remain ill, freeze in winter. And the measure of 'not enough' profit is whether *more* profit can be made by investing in something else— or just speculating in stocks or currencies or derivatives—gambling on futures, taking bets on what other speculators will gamble on. If this restaurant isn't making a profit, the investment goes somewhere else. Fair enough, maybe. But if a private hospital isn't making a profit, it closes. But what if *all* the restaurants and *all* the hospitals were unprofitable, compared with some financial ponzi scheme or a sub-prime mortgage scam? Then we would all be eating crisps—if we had any way to pay for them —

The waiter brings the bill to Andriy. Tom intercepts it.

       TOM
I'll get that, Andriy. This is on me.

       ROISIN *(irritated by all this)*
No, Tom. It's our treat. Our city.
Give it to Andriy.

ANDRIY *(smiles)*
It's our bill. We're capitalists, after all, Tom.

TOM *(laughs, breaking the mood)*
OK, my capitalist friends. Look, I'll do you a deal.
You can pay the bill *if* you can make money *make
more money* just by being passed from hand to hand.
Which is all that finance capital does these days.
It's not money that makes wealth happen, makes
extra value. It's only by actually making things—
and speculative finance capitalism doesn't do that,
even when it invests in people who do. So, Andriy,
here's a hundred koruna note. Without actually
making anything, see if you make it grow for us.
And then you can pay the bill with it.

ANDRIY *(no hesitation)*
Easy. Hand it over.

Tom looks at him!

ANDRIY *(with a flourish of his pen)*
I'll just sign it. As a well-known Prague artist.
Now it's worth *far* more than a hundred koruna.
I think I'll call it 'The Koruna—Number 3'. *(laughs)*
Picasso used to doodle on napkins or tablecloths, to
pay for his lunch, or just sign the bill! Fair enough?

TOM
OK, *touché*. T. S. Eliot was once at a dinner party.
His host proudly showed him a book signed by
Ezra Pound. Eliot, ever the gentleman, politely
asked "May I?" and then added his own signature.
"It's worth *twice* as much now," he said, handing it
back. *(laughs)* But that won't do, Andriy. That's not
capital—that's art. You've just *made* art. And you'd
still have to *sell* it. To the waiter? Try again. The bill
comes to 140 koruna by the way.

ANDRIY *(smiling, as he acts out the following:)*
Right, Tom, you seem to think a capitalist economy
consists of just workers and capitalists, in conflict.
A very old fashioned view. What about the banks?
So, I'm now a bank. And, thank you, you've just
deposited one hundred koruna with me, for which I
will pay you interest of one koruna. OK? Now, as a
responsible bank, I have to keep a sensible reserve,
say ten per cent, ten koruna, in cash. But I can lend
out the rest of your deposit. Yes? So I'm now
lending ninety koruna to Roisin.
(Hands her nine ten-koruna notes) For which I will
charge her two koruna interest. Yes? But she's also a
bank. So she gets the 90 koruna, and pays me the
two koruna, of which I pay your account one
koruna as your interest, then she puts 8 koruna on
reserve and lends you, or someone else, 82 koruna
at an interest rate of 3 koruna. *(he swaps notes and coins
round on the table like a card trick)* So: now *you* have
101 koruna in my bank, I also have assets of 101
koruna, 10 in reserve, 90 lent to Roisin, and 1
koruna overall interest, and Roisin has assets of 82
koruna lent to you, or someone else, with 3 koruna
still owed her as interest. That's a grand total
between us of 287 koruna. *Magic!* So now we can
easily pay the bill twice over. All we need is our
credit cards on our respective accounts. Which I'm
very happy to issue, as a respectable bank—but of
course with a supplementary charge or fee of two
koruna. There are expenses, you know—

ROISIN *(laughs delightedly)*
So we're paying the bill Tom!

WAITER *(who has been listening)*
But we do not accept credit cards, sir.

ANDRIY *(mock indignation)*
Regressive Socialistické! No tip for you.
(Hands him 150 koruna.) Just keep the change.

TOM *(gives up and laughs)*
You win! I can see why everything in Prague is
called 'Magic'. 'Magic Pizzeria'. 'Magic Hotel'.
'Magic Cafe'. Bring back the alchemists! —
Ah, but what if I want my 100 koruna back?

ANDRIY
I'll get a bailout from the state!
The tax payer will pay for our lunch!

ROISIN *(firmly)*
No more arguing, Tom. Some of us have to work,
after all. End of lunch-break! I have to go and open
the shop. Are you going back to the conference or
are you sightseeing?

TOM
Many thanks for lunch. *(pause)* I might just go back
to the Castle. I still haven't seen the Golden Lane
—it was far too crowded this morning. I'd kind of
like to see Kafka's writing cottage again, at least,
but the Lane was full of foreign tourists—like me,
I suppose.

ANDRIY
It will be like that all day, Tom It's a lot better after
six o'clock, when the day trippers have all gone—
and it's free then. And it's best of all late at night,
when the moon's out. Why not come back this
evening and we'll take you there.

TOM
Lovely idea. But this evening I've going to a party.
In fact, someone from that exciting era of
computing—Maria Kolar—one of the great
innovators. She did all that incredible early

software—pattern recognition, OCR, music
sampling—I didn't even know she was in Prague.
But she's a friend of a friend, so I'm invited to her
house tonight. You remember her?

ROISIN
Yes, Tom, she lives just up the hill from us.
But we've never actually met her. She's supposed to
be incredibly reclusive. The story is that she sold
her company right at the crest of the dot com
bubble—and made a simply fantastic killing.
But then she married the accountant who handled
the deal for her—and ended up programming
financial software—a pretty boring end to a great
career. Legendary in her day, of course, but another
one captured by commerce. Another capitalist! I
didn't think you would approve, Tom!

ANDRIY
Anyway, come after the party—just ring the side
door bell to the flat above the shop. Any time up to
about eleven. The Castle gets locked at midnight.

TOM
Sounds great. But that means I have to finish
writing my paper for tomorrow right now. This
afternoon. I normally leave it till the night before,
when panic and adrenalin kick in. And I'm currently
stuck. Not much to say. So, I need somewhere
quiet and peaceful for the rest of the afternoon,
preferably with a view. I might just stay here.
(looks around with after-lunch satisfaction)

ANDRIY
Ah, no, Tom — I have just the place for you—
ten minutes walk from here.

18. INT. VERY EXPENSIVE HOTEL ROOM.

Viktor is working on a laptop. Joe is standing, waiting.
Finally, Viktor gestures to Joe.

     VIKTOR *[subtitles]*
Oznámit! [Report!]

     JOE
Není policista. On je novinář. Na volné noze.
[He is not the police. He's a journalist. Freelance.]

     VIKTOR
Ví o tom něco?
[Does he know anything?]

     JOE
Možná. Díval se na některé z našich prodejen.
[Perhaps. He was looking at some of our outlets.]

     VIKTOR
Dohoda Basel je pozítří. Dostat ho z cesty. Ale ne
ho zabít. Aby to vypadalo jako loupež. Dnes v noci.
[The Basel deal is the day after tomorrow.
Get him out of the way. But don't kill him.
Make it look like a robbery. Do it tonight.]

19. EXT. LATE AFTERNOON.
TERRACE OF HANAVSKY PAVILION.

Tom is writing, long hand, in a notepad, with several empty coffee cups.
Not much has been written. He sips more coffee.

20. EXT. EVENING. SQUARE NEAR LORETO. OUTSIDE
A VERY OPULENT HOUSE: MARIA'S.

Don McKenzie is sitting at a pavement cafe, opposite the entrance to
Maria's house, taking covert photos with his phone-camera of those
going in. A number of men and women arrive and are ushered in by a
butler figure. They are mainly elderly.

Don's phone rings.

                    DON
Hi. What have you got for me? *(long pause)*
So the whole of Zymbio et Cie is changing hands.
(pause) Under the counter sale. Yes. But you don't
know who's really buying? *(long pause)* Brilliant.
Self-financing. Can you get the account details for
me? *(pause).* No, of course not. Don't email, and
don't ring this phone. Too easy to trace. *(thinks)*
Look, I can give you a different number.
Temporary. Use just this once. The phone has no
connection with me but I can access it.
Just text the account number. Nothing else. OK—

21. EXT. CONTINUOUS.

Joe is in the shadows nearby, observing Don,
but too far away to hear what he is saying.

22. INT. MARIA'S HOUSE. VERY OPULENT.

Tom and Stefan arrive together. They are shown into the large
ballroom, where about fifty people are drinking and talking round a
long buffet table. They are mainly men and almost all are elderly.
Maria comes over and greets them.

                    MARIA
Stefan. Tom Brady. So glad you could both come.
You've missed most of the food and drink, I'm
afraid. Many of my guests have early bedtimes!
We're about to start the presentations, but do make
sure you have a glass with me afterwards.

The butler sounds a small gong and everybody drifts into the next room,
a large drawing room, with chairs in rows and a presentation screen
at one end. Maria has a remote control for the slide presentation.

MARIA

Good evening everybody. Welcome to the League
of Alchemists monthly report. I'll keep it brief as
usual. First, let us remember with respect this
month's deceased members and their legacies.

She clicks the remote control and a Power Point slide shows the
following:

LEGACIES: 6 MEMBERS: €239 MILLION

After a silent pause, there is subdued applause from the audience.
Then Maria initiates a sequence of slides showing:

EMERGENCY APPEAL DONATIONS: €42M
CHARITY AUCTION BIDS: € 28M
 WALKS & EVENTS SPONSORSHIP: €14M.
DIRECT MEMBERS' DONATIONS: €178M

A slide stays on longer than the others, showing:

SOME NEW BENEFICIARIES TO CONSIDER

Race on the Agenda; Female Prisoners Welfare
Project Hibiscus; The Africa Book Campaign;
Enfants du Monde – Droits de l'Homme; Comfort
Rwanda - Street Kids Rescue; Kakai Sand Dam;
Malaika Kids Relatives Support Programme;
Gesellschaft für das Gute und Gemeinnützige;
Mkurangu children's village; Maendeleo Agricultural
Enterprise Fund; Guangzhou Huiling; Lifeline;
Environmental Justice in Cameroon; Télécoms sans
frontières; Water for Enkito; JAM Mozambique
Deworming project; Afghanaid; African Caribbean
Leukaemia Trust; Medair UK.

Lists of all beneficiaries available in the Library.

The final slide shows :

CURRENT TOTAL: €3,680 MILLION.
ANNUAL TARGET: €12 BILLION

MARIA *(leaves the last slide up as she speaks)*
As you can see, ladies and gentlemen, I'm afraid this
is sadly disappointing. We are unfortunately falling
ever further behind our revised donations target.
The daily income is still increasing quite drastically,
so the surplus balance is almost getting out of hand.
Despite your best efforts, we must do even better.
Your management committee has been trying to
devise new procedures and tactics, but our recent
pilot projects have not been very successful.
The suggestion of donating designer dresses to
charity shops yielded only a limited million or so,
about the same as the anonymous donation last
month of rare first editions to Oxfam bookshops.
We will of course look again at variations on this
current idea, but we are rather desperate for more
input. Suggestions, please, to the committee.
We urgently need more ideas on how to make
more and bigger ad hoc donations.
You will find this month's cash injections in the
billiards room. There is more than usual, so I hope
you will take as much as you can deliver discreetly.
Do please remember to keep below the relevant tax
radar in your respective countries. And please make
sure your accounts and wills are fully up to date.
The League accountant and lawyer are available as
usual in the study. The Dignitas panel is in the front
drawing room.
I will be in the library if a member has any particular
or confidential business to raise with me.
Do enjoy the rest of the evening, as much as you
can, and as many as possible of us will meet again
next month, on a date to be arranged in the usual
way. And thank you so much for all your good
work. Do keep it up for as long as you are able.

People drift into the billiards room, where Maria's two suitcases from the station lie open on the billiard table. They are full of bundles of hundred euro notes. Chatting casually to each other, mainly about illnesses, people methodically help themselves to the money, putting bundles into carrier bags, briefcases, shoulder bags, handbags.

Tom is looking on amazed.

>   STEFAN
> Well, Tom, I suppose you want to know more.

>   TOM
> You bet!

>   STEFAN
> So, let's join Maria in the library.

23. INTERIOR. LIBRARY.

Maria serves glasses of wine to Tom and Stefan.

>   MARIA
> Tom, Stefan tells me your heart is in the right place.
> But your brain has some major problems.
> That's one reason you were invited here tonight.
> We always need new members in the League of
> Alchemists. We hope you might be interested in
> joining. I gather you may only have six months or
> so left. And you have no dependants. Exactly what
> we always look for. In addition, you actually are the
> Tom Brady who used to write so optimistically
> about the future of computing, as I thought, yes?
> So perhaps you will be especially sympathetic to
> what we are doing.

24. EXT. LATE EVENING. OUTSIDE MARIA'S HOUSE.

Some guests are leaving, with their various loaded bags.
Don is still there taking surreptitious photos.

25. INT. LIBRARY.

MARIA *(has been explaining)*
— So we began by recruiting people who would
leave some of our money in their will to whatever
good causes they themselves favoured. With the
right choice of people, we found that even very
large amounts left to charities tend not to be
challenged or the will queried. Once a person is
dead, if they have no family or dependants, nobody
is in a position normally to claim that the money
was somehow left to the wrong causes, or owing to
them, or even to the tax man. It's also quite hard to
investigate if you do it properly. But of course,
given the people we invite to join, we have, shall we
say, a constant turn-over of members. Though such
people are often likely to know others in the same
unfortunate situation. We recruit mainly through
personal contact.

TOM
I can see where this enormous wealth came from —
after all, I know the story of Maria Kolar and the
dot com bubble—but I don't really understand.
Why not just give it away yourself, or set up a trust
or a foundation?

MARIA
Well, let us just say for now that the story of the dot
com bubble isn't quite accurate. Yes, I did make a
great deal of money by floating Kolar Inc. just at the
right moment. Thanks to my late husband.
My accountant. But also thanks to him, I then,
shall we say, changed my field of interest and
together we developed an interesting little suite of
programs. You see, every financial and commercial
company in the world is heavily involved in foreign
currency exchange—whether just buying or selling
products in foreign markets, importing and
exporting, or lending and borrowing across

currency frontiers, or just using overnight inter-
bank loans between global domains. For a decade
or so large internationals like Sony, for example,
have made more regular profit from overnight
currency swaps than from actually manufacturing
anything. But those operations take place while
exchange rates themselves are often adjusting in
very rapid movements, reciprocally. So keeping
track of deals made across several currencies
while those currencies themselves are fluctuating,
however minutely or otherwise, involves quite
complex software—which has to handle huge
quantities of currency flows while tracking micro-
second feedback alterations between several
different currencies at once—and effectively that
software has to be standardised across the entire
range of global transactions. So that's what we
developed, my husband and I. Our programs are
now used in almost every large transaction involving
foreign currency exchanges. Now let that sink in.

TOM

Yes, I do get the point. There must be exchanges
involving several trillion dollars, pounds, euros,
whatever, every twenty-four hours. Billions every
minute even.

MARIA

And, naturally, we built into the programs that our
company receives a fixed fee for every single
transaction. Just a miniscule, infinitesimal, almost
invisible fee. Not quite zero. But it does mount up.

TOM

I bet it does!

MARIA

It's not even a bet, Tom. Unlike many of the
transactions themselves. But as the financial
markets, exploded from 2000 onwards, our fee

income became almost unmanageable. Asymptotic!
And again, after the banking debacle in 2008,
transactions multiplied even more, as banks and
others tried to shift huge sums of money around the
globe, looking for safe havens, however temporary.
But what were we to do with our own increasing
income from those transaction fees? As the man
said, there are only so many meals you can eat.
Yet how could we even think about investing that
amount without destabilising the very system we
were servicing? We decided the only thing we could
do was to give it away. But if we set up a public
fund or charitable organisation we would become
one of the biggest players on the planet. Every
cause, every agency, every NGO, every charity,
every individual, would want to make requests,
demands, calls upon us. And how would we decide
between them? Did we want to become yet another
powerful agency choosing our own priorities—
which might well be misguided? *(pause)* In the end,
we decided to let ordinary people decide for us.
And especially people who had very little to gain for
themselves from making decisions about such very
large sums of money. Which is why we looked for
those about to die. *(pause)* Those with no family or
dependants. People who would think about
what is to come after them, but not what would
benefit them or their own children directly.
And after the changes in 1989 there were very many
people of a certain age who had once had ideals for
the future of a more equal and just society,
but who now had no belief in the new world order.
We started with them.

    TOM
Which is how you became involved, Stefan?
From your involvement with Solidarnosce in the
early days? And then your terminal diagnosis?

STEFAN

Spot on, Tom—but then I actually survived my cancer! Perhaps I should have been more careful! It's been hell these past few years trying to decide what best to do with a few billion—it's not too bad if you think you only have to make those decisions for your last few months at most. And then, literally, leave it all behind you. But making such decisions every month is a strain, I can tell you.

TOM

I'm staggered. So, how does it all work? I saw the money on the billiard table this evening—but that's hardly the way to shift millions, let alone billions.

MARIA

No, no, of course not, that's just for petty cash donations, being stopped in the street by charity muggers, dropping wads of cash into collecting boxes, that kind of thing. The usual way is that each member has a number of Swiss bank accounts, which the League sets up, and they make bank transfers in relatively small amounts, say up to fifty thousand dollars a time—but to lots of different charities, mainly small ones. So long as all those charities don't make the cross-connections, and realise that the same donor is giving to lots of them, the donations don't attract much attention outside the individual charities—and of course, most of the donations are made on conditions of strict anonymity. There are over seven thousand charities listed on just one of the donor information websites we funded, in just one country. Multiply that by pretty well every country and you have a wide choice. And then the final big donations come in the members' wills, posthumously, and they mainly go to the very large charity and aid organisations.

STEFAN

As it happens, though, Prague is quite handy for
distributing cash, even quite a lot of cash. Maria
goes to Basel once a month, where the League's
main banks are, to keep tabs on the League's
accounts as people die, and to set up new ones for
new members—and Swiss law allows you to take
out or bring in as much actual cash as you like—
as well as offering that famous Swiss bank secrecy.
And if you travel by train the only searches are for
drugs—once the cash is inside the EU there are
effectively no border restrictions on currency
movements, so people can go back with lots of cash
to their various European countries, without too
much bother.

MARIA

And of course, people can come to Prague quite
casually—there's always visitors, tourists, and so on.
Nobody notices a few elderly people meeting once a
month. So we can get together easily. There's quite a
lot of administration, which the various committees
will do tomorrow. And of course even experienced
committee members don't last very long. We
haven't fully cracked the problem of expanding
outside Europe yet, but obviously we now have a
network of members all over the globe. But we still
rely largely on existing members to recommend
recruits. So far we've been very fortunate.

STEFAN

But we barely make a dent, even so. We estimate it
would only take about 200 billion US dollars a year
to eradicate world poverty within a decade.
A small percentage of the global military budgets.
But that would have to be done not by lots of
charity donations from dying old age pensioners but
by major changes in global government policies.
Especially on tax avoidance. At the moment, the

really ultra-rich, a tiny tiny number of individuals
have, according to our best estimates, about eleven
trillion dollars in off-shore assets, earning an untaxed
income of about eight hundred billion a year.
The unpaid annual tax just on that income alone
could be more than the two hundred billion needed.

     MARIA
At least whenever they move their wealth offshore
they probably pay us a currency exchange fee.
But given the scale of the problems, and the fact
that we really don't make all that much difference,
we are trying very hard to think of further ways and
means.

     TOM
My brain is still reeling—and it's not just the
tumour, which hardly seems important right now.
Look, I do want to know more—but I have a
promise to keep at the moment. I'm due to meet
some friends nearby. Can I think about all this and
come round tomorrow, after my conference paper?
Or maybe just talk more to Stefan? I can see you
back at the hotel, Stefan, yes?

     MARIA
That's fine, Tom. Yes, talk to Stefan tomorrow.
And we can certainly meet again in a day or so,
before you leave Prague.

26. EXT. OUTSIDE MARIA'S HOUSE. NIGHT.

*Tom leaves the house, and walks thoughtfully down towards the castle.
Don quietly follows him. And Joe very quietly follows Don.*

27. EXT. A STREET NEAR THE CASTLE.

*Don is attacked by two men and badly beaten up.
They take a wallet and phone from him. He is left in the roadway.*

28. EXT. IN THE GOLDEN LANE. MOONLIGHT.

Andriy takes a photo of Roisin and Tom standing outside the Kafka cottage.

> ANDRIY
>
> There, now you've definitely been to Prague. You have the evidence to prove it! The Alchemists Lane. And Kafka's Cottage. *(smiles)* But there were never really alchemists in the lane. Goldsmiths Lane is more accurate. This is where the goldsmiths worked, on real wealth not fantasies.

> TOM *(very subdued)*
>
> Only if you believe in gold as real wealth, Andriy. Remember in More's *Utopia* they make prisoners' chains out of it. And toilets!

> ANDRIY
>
> Granted. But Emperor Rudolf wasn't really interested in making a golden fortune anyway. He had one already. And in any case he thought what was really of value were all those relics and bones of saints. His most precious items were two nails from Christ's cross! What he was interested in was *predicting* his fortune, not making one. Not alchemists but astrologers. Not gold but the future. That's what he mainly employed John Dee and Kelly for. Casting horoscopes. But of course their science of astrology, of fore-telling men's fates from the movements of the stars, wasn't real science at all. That was happening just over the Castle hill. Tycho Brahe in his observatory, meticulously recording the exact positions of the stars and planets, night after night. Looking up at these very same skies.

He points and they look up at the sky.
Then they talk as they stroll back through the castle grounds.
Andriy and Roisin try to arouse Tom's interest
but he remains silent, preoccupied.

ROISIN

— Then Kepler comes to Prague, and laboriously
calculates the mathematical relations between those
heavenly positions—and ends up with his laws of
planetary motion. Tycho Brahe still thought the sun
went round the earth, but his work and Kepler's
cleared the way for Galileo's telescope and for
proving that Copernicus was right after all.
It was Prague where astrology really began to give
way to astronomy.

ANDRIY

So, not really an alchemists lane at all, Tom.
The old framework of occult powers and hidden
forces shaping our fortunes yielded to scientific
observation and scientific laws right here.
You can predict the position of a new planet and
find it. But you can't predict a man's fate. No more
Fortuna, no more horoscopes, no more Lady Luck!

ROISIN

Not so fast, Andriy. Remember we still have to sell
our Tarot cards! It isn't as simple as that anyway.
For a start, those precise astronomical calculations
are ultimately based on sheer cosmic chance—what
are the infinite odds on human beings even existing,
let alone becoming astronomers!—and on quantum
statistics, on random fluctuations. Science can't
really predict reality at the deepest level. So maybe
there really are other levels and kinds of reality than
our science can deal with. Call it magic if you like.
But people haven't given up believing in fate and
chance and luck. Why do they gamble on the stock
exchange or buy a lottery ticket? Not because
there's any really scientific way of predicting the
movements of individual shares, or even large-scale
patterns in the markets—however hard the
mathematical wide-boys, the Quants, tried in the
days before 2008. Statistics can tell you there will be
fifteen winners on the week's lottery—but not *which*
individual will suddenly become incredibly wealthy.

People still think some share-dealers do have a
magic touch—an intuition, a hunch, a gambler's
nose. And they're right.

ANDRIY *(laughs)*
Tycho Brahe had a golden nose. Did that help him?

ROISIN *(concerned)*
Tom, you've been very quiet. Not like you to stay
out of a good argument! Or are you just going to
defend good old marxist determinism?

TOM *(smiles but is still distracted)*
Nope. At the end of his life, Marx tried to teach
himself the calculus, because he thought the kind of
maths used to understand economics was pretty
inadequate. Most neo-classicial economic theory is
still based on 1860s maths—and it doesn't work.
Like Poincaré's eventual solution to the gaps in
Kepler's planetary motion laws, economics needs
dynamic not linear mathematics. Sorry. *(pause)*
But I was thinking of something completely
different. What if you *did* win the lottery?
What if, like Kafka's Gregor in the tale he wrote
back there in his sister's cottage in the Golden Lane,
you woke up one morning to find you'd been
miraculously metamorphosed—into a fabulously
wealthy individual—by a kind of chance, luck,
whatever. What would you spend it on? And how?

*They have reached the outer courtyard—and the guard has just closed
the main gates. It is midnight. Andriy sees this and sprints towards
the gate. Roisin and Tom follow him.*

ANDRIY
Please. Open the gate! We're tourists!

GUARD *(a large Kafkaesque figure...)*
Musíte jít na druhou stranu.
[You must go out the other way.]

ANDRIY
That's a very long way round!

GUARD
Ah, a 'tourist' who understands Czeck. So go the
long way round. This gate is now closed to you.

Roisin and Tom arrive.

ROISIN
Did you know that 'Praha' means doorstep,
threshold, gateway—welcome to Praha.
This could be interesting. *(she gestures behind her)*

*Behind them across the courtyard come six English yobbos waving
bottles of Pilsner and singing. The Guard takes one long look.
Hesitates. Then he opens the gate.*

ANDRIY
Děkuju mnohokrát. Budete odměněni v nebi.
[Thank you very much. You will be rewarded in
heaven.]

GUARD *glares at him.*

As they pass through:

TOM *(very subdued)*
Look, I have something to tell you both.
Share with you. Ask you about. A problem.
Can we please go back to the flat for a while?

29. INT. HOSPITAL. PRIVATE ROOM.

*[Hospital: Nemocnice Milosrdných Sester sv. Karla Boromejského V
Praze, Vlašská 336/36, 118 00 Praha 1-Malá Strana]*
*Don is lying in a hospital bed, unconscious. His head is bandaged.
A nurse is in attendance. A police officer is standing by the bed,
looking through a wallet he has taken from Don's jacket.
He calls in on his police radio.*

POLICE OFFICER

Jméno oběti je Thomas Brady. Angličtina. K
dispozici je kreditní karta. Visa 489846530842.
Zkontrolujte hotely, pokud můžete. OK?
[The name of the victim is Thomas Brady. English.
There is a credit card. Visa 489846530842.
Check hotels if you can. OK?]

30. INT. VIKTOR'S HOTEL ROOM.

Viktor is looking through Don's own wallet and phone.
Rudy is working on a laptop.

VIKTOR *(subtitles)*

Má vymazány své telefonní hovory pro dnešek.
Zajímavé. Uvidíme, jestli naši lidé mohou dostat
zpět. A kdo jsou všichni ti lidé, on fotografoval?
Proč?
[He's wiped his phone calls for today. Interesting.
See if our people can recover them. And who are all
these people he photographed? Why?]

31. INT. FLAT ABOVE SHOP. AFTER MIDNIGHT.

Roisin, Andriy and Tom are into their second bottle of wine.
Tom has been explaining about Maria and about his own tumour.
They are fairly subdued and sober despite the wine.

ANDRIY

I think I have a partial solution to Maria's problems.
Some of them anyway. Remember I was a well-
trained Soviet hacker before I became a Western
capitalist! I'll have to think it through, see if it's
really possible. But I think she can simply transfer
large funds without leaving any trace of origin at all.
She won't even need to recruit dying old age
pensioners—she could just create virtual ones,
making huge but untraceable donations.
Admittedly, that puts the decisions about who to
give the money to back into her own hands.

                    ROISIN

But that isn't the only issue, is it Tom? I don't really
buy her story about the tiny transaction fee.
I have one of those hunches—*(Andriy laughs quietly)*
I suspect we're actually dealing with a money-
laundering operation. Illegal money. *That*'s why she
won't go public with a fund or charitable
foundation. Prague isn't just renowned for its
pickpockets. They're small fry. It's also a prime
place for international money laundering.
That's why she's in Prague. The poor old Czech
koruna still has its uses, as a threshold between, say,
Russia and the Eurozone. I suspect that's one
reason we've still got this currency. Andriy can tell
you.

                    ANDRIY

Yes. One favourite laundering channel is all those
art galleries you see around the place. Most of them
are owned by Russians. But you don't think they
actually sell all those terrible pictures to tourists with
no taste. But it's very easy to 'sell' a painting for
whatever your accountant says you can get away
with. So you pay an 'artist' 50 koruna for just one
grotty daub. Then 'sell' it, on paper, for 5,000
rubles. Imported Mafia cash roubles. And then you
'sell ' it again and again, under different titles if you
like. Which tax authority is going to track down an
alleged passing tourist who paid cash and has taken
his nice souvenir painting of the Charles Bridge
back to Rumania, or Israel, or Connecticut—even if
there ever was any such art-loving dope in the first
place. And, of course, you can bank each 'sale' in
roubles or whatever cash currency you like, but then
draw it out of the bank in Euros. Magic! If nobody
looks too closely. Maria may be just operating on a
much bigger scale, using dying dupes rather than
dubious artists and gullible or ghost tourists.

TOM

You may be right. I just don't know. But there's
another aspect to the whole problem, which
interests me. If you really did have that much
money to dispose of for good causes, need it be a
matter of trying to use it for good causes *within* the
system. Or might you actually have the leverage to
change the system as a whole? Is that possible?

ROISIN

I don't follow you.

TOM

Two things are worrying away at me. The first is
simple. Remember the Connection Machine, the
fastest computer of its time —designed by Daniel
Hillis—he once described being a computer
designer as inscribing runes on a stone and then
asking it questions—a kind of magic he would have
been burned for in the old days. We know it's not
magic. But does it have magical potential?
Second, we're living through another great
Copernican transformation. Not from astrology to
astronomy, but from gold to credit cards to digital
debt, from industrial capitalism through global
financial capitalism to whatever is emerging as a
purely digital economy on a quite different basis.
The old capitalist world used to revolve round
manufacturing, with investment as simply how the
money went into manufacturing, to get a surplus
value, a profit, out of the product when it was sold.
But now 'investment' is itself the glorious sun
around which every other aspect of the economic
world revolves. And investment itself revolves
round the big black hole of credit, not product.
Banks are now the gravitational centre of the global
system. And at the heart of banks is not gold but
numbers, ones and zeroes, digital records.
You don't put money into a factory any more,
where you might get a mere 3 per cent return;

you 'borrow' thirty times the money you have—
which means you simply multiply your account
numbers by thirty—and gamble that virtual money
on something which may be entirely without social
usefulness, but which gives you at least 6 per cent
return, or a great deal more. Like a credit default
swap on a currency devaluation, or a hedged bet on
the future price of corn. All done with computers,
and often with automated programs that trigger
instant transactions. But can computerisation,
the digital economy, also be today's white magic?
Can we make it so? Does Maria's wealth maybe
make it possible? You were saying earlier tonight
that Prague was once the threshold between
astrology and astronomy. Well, it was also once,
briefly, back in '68, hovering on the threshold
between a bankrupt order and a new socialism—
one with a human face. I still look back to that
moment.

        ANDRIY *(slightly drunk)*
We're just having one of those drunken late-night
student exchanges. Like the good old days.

        ROISIN
No. Spell it out, Tom. Tell us what you're driving at.

        TOM
Remember the old socialist arguments about
successive economic forms, ways of life The long
hunting and agricultural ages, several millenia
entirely based upon the scarce resources of land and
life, including raw materials, animals and labour,
physical muscles, some basic material tools.
But then the extraordinary rapid development of
mechanically manufactured objects, inert raw
material transformed by labour, now including
massive mechanical muscle, plus 'capital' — but

conflict and scarcity were, and still are, endemic in that form of organisation of physical production: unfairness, systematic unequal exchange, and exploitation. Competition. What is mine isn't yours.

ANDRIY
Unless we share it. Have another drink, Tom—

TOM
But it's no longer just sharing or some kind of cooperative. In a digital economy that basic competitive rule need not apply. What is mine can *also* be yours. We can make as many identical *copies* as we like of all those objects which can take a digital form. At very little cost in terms of the previous economies. But at present we are in-between. We are in financial capitalism.
We effectively already have a digital money economy —we can create as much credit as we like—call it quantitative easing or leveraged borrowing or fiat money, but it's basically making digital or virtual copies of banknotes—but this is now disconnected from what used to be called the real economy, the actual production of things for use. And the effects of that second phase are still with us—since the accumulation of enormous wealth which underpins financial capitalism was and is at the expense of the majority of people—and now most people don't earn enough within that older economy, that segment of the overall capitalist system, to be able to buy even the necessary goods produced by that system. So manufacturing capitalism regularly goes into crisis, or grinds to a halt in over-production and under-employment—unless, crucially, people buy on credit, go into debt—and thereby become integral to the financial form of capitalism.

ROISIN
But you can't have a fully digital economy—
you can't make digital food.

ANDRIY
Or digital wine—

TOM
Let me come back to that. Look, the current
proliferation of debt only displaces the crisis to
repeating itself some time into the future. When the
credit boom collapses, once again. Because we can
never produce enough real wealth to pay off these
virtual debts. And meanwhile the overall notional
wealth, all those enormous sums of money, the
profits of the previous gambling cycle, have to be
somehow 're-invested' yet again—to get the 'highest
rate of return' even if that means polluting the
planet, choking the atmosphere, sponsoring wars
causing famines, strangling the globe. And turning
absolutely everything into a commodity with an
increasingly arbitrary price. Like this season's over-
priced must-have consumer goods which will be
almost worthless when their brief reign of fame and
advertised desirability is over. Prague itself is now a
case of almost terminal tourism—it's a city where
more and more people who live in it are only
employed to make things, experiences, services, for
other people who don't live in it, but who come to
the place precisely for those manufactured
experiences, services, things. At an arbitrary price.
A postcard of an illuminated Prague Castle for five
dollars. And like any other brand-name or fashion,
trendy artist or overnight music sensation, it will be
replaced in due course. Leaving not a wrack of real
economy behind. But if the crazy accumulation of
money has created these issues, can some of it help
not just to palliate the effects but to transform
them? Maria's crazy wealth comes just from a side-
effect of global currency exchanges, and she's only

slicing off the margins of an entire system. But can
we use her money and the power of computers
combined to *change* that system?

ANDRIY *(getting drunk)*
Maybe she should pay off the credit card debts of
everybody on the planet? Including mine. Or pay
off all third world government debts. A debt jubilee!
I'll vote for that! Or—Well, maybe she already has
the best idea. Just give it to organisations doing real
jobs, those which pick up the shattered pieces.

ROISIN *(has been thinking)*
A question. What happens to the money paid for a
really good painting if the painting is destroyed?
Somebody pays ten million for a Picasso. For his
signature, if you like. That ten million goes to
someone else. But then the painting is burned in a
fire. Has ten million now disappeared from the
system? Or what if the painting is found to be a
fake? And what happens if you just erase those
ones and zeroes in a bank account? Is it like losing
heavily on a bad investment? Can money simply
disappear? Magicked away? You had 100 million in
shares. Great crash. Company collapses. You now
have ten million. Or nothing?

TOM
—Nothing except a fake Picasso! I'm not sure I can
see where you're going, Roisin—but I need to crash
out myself. I've just remembered that I still haven't
finished my conference paper for tomorrow.
Can I stay here tonight and get up early to scribble
something in time. I'm going to have major anxiety
dreams as it is.

ANDRIY
There's a spare room, yes. Free. No problem.

—Did you know. Tom, it was a professional
magician who opened the first cinema in Prague?
They thought films were magic. I still do.

                TOM
I like that. Not sure it helps. But I'll sleep on it.

32. INT. HOTEL LOBBY. MORNING.

A (different) Police Officer is talking to Stefan Mazur in the lobby.

                POLICE OFFICER
The hotel manager tells me, Professor Mazur, that
you left the hotel with Professor Brady yesterday
evening and that you returned alone late at night.
Can you tell me anything more, sir?

                STEFAN
Yes, indeed. We both went to a small private party
near the Castle. Professor Brady left at about ten,
 to see some friends nearby. I didn't see him again.
How badly injured is he?

                POLICE OFFICER
He's still unconscious, but it's not life-threatening.
But we would be grateful if you would come and
formally identify him for us. There's a small puzzle.
His wallet contained his credit cards. But he had
reported them stolen. Do you know anything about
that, sir?

                STEFAN
Well, he told me he had his wallet stolen at the
station. I'll certainly come to the hospital. But first
I must alert the conference organisers—Professor
Brady was due to give a lecture in about half an
hour. They'll have to make other arrangements at
very short notice. And I think I'd better alert our
hostess from last night. She will be very concerned.

She can meet us at the hospital. Let me make some
phone calls.

33. FLAT ABOVE SHOP.

*Tom is sitting glumly over a black coffee, looking pretty wretched.
Andriy enters, cheerful.*

> ANDRIY
> Roisin and I stayed up most of the night.
> And we've got some possible ideas for Maria.
> Can you arrange for us to meet her? I'll fill you in --

> TOM
> Not now, please, Andriy. I still don't have a lecture
> to give. There's just *nothing* I want to say about *Faust*
> or *Timon of Athens* any more. Damn it. I'll just have
> to wing it. It'll take a miracle to save me from total
> humiliation and embarrassment. And my last-ever
> conference paper, too. Look, I'm going to catch a
> tram. I'll ring you later. Oh, damn, no phone!

34. EXT. KARMELITSKA STREET.

*Tom is on a 57 tram heading south, face furrowed with thought.
Suddenly he thinks he spots Stefan in the back of a police car
speeding north. He shakes his head.*

> TOM *(mutters)*
> What's the Czech for a lousy hangover?

35. INT. LARGE CONFERENCE HALL.

*Professor Sorge is a long-suffering Conference Organiser and is making
a reluctant announcement from the stage to a crowded lecture theatre.*

> SORGE
> I am very sorry to tell you that our first speaker this
> morning, Professor Tom Brady, is unable to be
> with us. Again.

He is, we believe, in hospital after an unfortunate
accident. But not seriously injured. However, I am
happy to say that Professor Çapan has generously
agreed at very short notice to step into his shoes
and will be speaking to us about—

*As the announcement began Tom has entered in a rush from the rear of
the lecture theatre, fairly dishevelled and unshaven. He hears the
announcement. Stops dead. Sorge now spots him. Hesitates.
Then shouts across the hall.*

        SORGE
Tom, you made it. I thought you were in hospital?

        TOM
*(Totally bewildered at this, but sees his last chance — and
plays it even more bewildered.)* Er, yes. Just got out.
Not very well. Er, which hospital? Was I in?

        SORGE *(baffled)*
Nemocnice Milosrdných Sester sv. Karla
Boromejského.

        TOM *(shouts)*
The *what?*

        DELEGATE
*(a local Czech delegate, sitting near where Tom is standing,
whispers:)* Are you drunk? The Sisters of Charity.
On Vlašská Street.

        TOM
Ah, right. Sorry. Got to get back. Find out how I
am. It's all right, everybody. I'll take a taxi. 'Bye.

*Tom exits rapidly. Sorge looks baffled but is resignedly used to this
kind of lunacy at academic conferences.*

36. HOSPITAL ROOM

Don is in bed, still bandaged. He is faking being asleep while listening to a Police Officer and Stefan and Maria talking together. This Police Officer has limited English and limited interest in this routine case.

> MARIA
>
> Yes, we say again that this man is *not* Tom Brady. God, I wish I knew Czech better. Er. Ano, řekl, že tento muž není Tom Brady. His wallet was stolen at the railway station. But I have never seen *this* man before. Jeho peněženka byla kradena na nádraží. Ale já jsem nikdy neviděl toho muže předtím. Ačkoli jeho tvář se zdá seznámeni. — But his face seems familiar.

Tom arrives in a hurry. Still hung over and fairly baffled.

> STEFAN
>
> *This* is Tom Brady.

> POLICE OFFICER.
>
> You know him? How long?

> STEFAN
>
> For twenty years.

Don pretends to suddenly wake up.
Immediately looks as if he is very pleased to see Tom.
Greets him loudly as an old friend.

> DON
>
> Is that old Tom? Tom! Oh, am I *so* glad to see you. It's Don, Don McKenzie. I got your wallet and phone back for you. I followed that damn pickpocket—but I got beaten up by his mates. *(gestures feebly).* Come a bit nearer, old buddy. Got something very important to tell you—

*Tom looks even more baffled, but succumbs. Tom bends down close,
over the recumbent Don, who grips his arm and whispers sotto voce :*

DON
I'm a British journalist. *Guardian.* So trust me.
Go along with it. Get rid of the police, for God's
sake. Take a gamble. It's important.

Tom straightens up, shrugs slightly at Maria and Stefan.

TOM
It's alright, officer. I can see how the mistake
happened. Don is an old friend I was hoping to
meet at the station. But I must have missed him.
He says he pursued the pickpocket—that's why he's
got my wallet. Er, everything's fine, just fine.

POLICE OFFICER
I must still take a statement. Regulations. The Law.

MARIA *(takes firm charge)*
In due course, officer. I think now that we've
established what happened, Mr McKenzie ought to
be left in peace with his friend for now. I'm sure
you could do with a break. Let me pay for a coffee,
or two, for you —Er, Jsem si jistý, co můžete udělat
s přestávkou. Dovolte mi, abych platit za kávy nebo
dvě pro vás . Now, how much is coffee? Kolik je
káva? *(gives him a very large note and ushers him out of the
room)*

POLICE OFFICER *(looks at banknote)*
Velmi dobrá káva! [Very good coffee!]

MARIA
We can call you when—

*As soon as the police officer leaves the room, Don is alert, but not
entirely recovered from concussion. Slightly manic.*

DON

Very sorry everybody. It's all a bit complicated.
But you can trust me. I work for the *Guardian*.
Right? It wasn't your pickpocket did this to me.
Though I did take Tom's wallet and phone off the
pickpocket who stole them. A couple of Mafia
thugs have been following me and did me over.
And they took my own wallet and my phone.
On that phone are photos of all your guests last
night, Mrs Kolar. I'm very sorry about that.
I'll explain why in a minute. But it may put them in
some danger. Though I don't think my Mafia thugs
will be able to work out what they—or you—are up
to. I haven't quite figured that out myself. And it
was only by accident that I even got involved with
the Mafia in the first place. But now I have
something I have to ask Tom Brady to help me
with. It's very urgent—

MARIA *(firmly interrupts)*

Just one moment, Mr McKenzie. You will have to
give us a rather clearer explanation than that. So you
don't actually know Tom Brady at all. But you do
know who I am, and you were spying on my little
party last night . Is that right? Why?

DON

OK, briefly. I was working on a story—I'd been
investigating the Koch brothers, and other secretive
billionaires who finance right wing groups in the
States, but all that was old hat—so I was pretty
pleased when I came across hints of some sort of
parallel outfit, that secretly funds left-wing causes,
liberal organisations, bleeding-heart NGOs, and so
on. *Guardian* types, you know. Just up their street.
Good scoop, maybe. So I traced that second
funding source to a bank in Basel, where I have—
well, anyway, that led me to you, Mrs Kolar.

But then I also came across a different story, about
Russian and Czech money laundering. In the good
old days I used to be an East European
correspondent, so I can recognise a mafia goon a
mile away. And this different story began to
interest me. So, if you can help me, or Tom does,
on *that* story, I'll agree to sort of forget the first
story—drop the story about yourself. Is it a deal?

      TOM
This is crazy. You want me to help you? How?.

      DON
I said they took my phone. But I always back up call
data and messages to the London office and
promptly wipe them off the phone. So I'm not too
worried about my Basel contact being traced. Look,
I'm just sorry I hadn't backed up those photos yet.
And wiped them. But thanks to your pickpocket,
I also had access to Tom's phone, which nobody
could connect with me. So I took the liberty of
using that just once, for my Basel contact to give me
some crucial information. And I need that
information right now. I need your phone.

      TOM *(still baffled)*
So where the hell is my phone?

      DON
In my hotel room.

      TOM
So you want me to go to your hotel room and get
my phone? Is that it?

      DON
No. I just want to ring it and access it. I need to
read a text message on it. Professor Stefan,

can you lend me your phone for a moment, and
Tom, can you give me your remote access code,
assuming you've changed it.

                    TOM
I never did. It's still the default. Whatever that is.

                    DON
Christ! When will people learn! Fine. A doddle.
No problem then. I don't need you. I just need a
phone. Stefan?

Stefan rather reluctantly hands him his phone.
Don punches away for a while. Then reads a message. Memorises it.

                    DON
Right, I've—

Stefan suddenly snatches the phone back before Don can erase the
transferred text message.

                    STEFAN
Didn't know you could do that.

                    DON
 I work for the *Guardian*, mate, not the *Sun*.
They don't know half the tricks.

                    TOM
Do I get my phone back now?
                    MARIA *(taking charge)*
I still think we need to know a lot more, Mr
Guardian McKenzie. Or I at least will be changing
my part of the story to that nice policeman—
So what is this text message you need so badly?
Explain as clearly as you can. Please.

DON

Fair enough. Basic point is that I need to make a
call to the Swiss banking authorities. Viktor—let's
call him Viktor—has run a regular laundering
operation through Prague and other cities, fairly
small stuff, channelled through art galleries, betting
shops, currency exchanges, and so on—every
month he or one of his goons would make the run
to Basel to put the toxic cash into a legit bank
account, before it got transferred back as clean
money to its original masters. Because Viktor
wasn't acting for himself. Oh no, behind him are
some pretty powerful figures, I can tell you.
Well, I spotted him at the station when I was
watching out for you, Mrs Kolar. But this month
they had a new job for him in Basel. According to
my inside source, he's about to use his own
account, massively leveraged by a temporary
transfer of funds from those very figures, to buy the
whole Basel bank outright —using the funds now
deposited in the bank itself. How neat is that!
A completely under the counter deal. But it will give
Viktor's masters a legitimate bank of some size, and
the control of a lot of connections and other
accounts—which will make their laundering a whole
lot easier. And give them even more leverage in the
future. Of course, you can buy and sell American
banks like toffee apples—there's even a website for
it—but Swiss banks are a bit different. The Swiss
have pretty tight regulations on bank ownership.
So I'm after a good juicy story—I want to alert the
Swiss banking authorities that a possibly illegal bank
purchase is about to happen—and for that they will
need access to Viktor's account—and it's the
number of *that* account I've just downloaded from
Tom's phone. As always, the best way to rob a bank
is to own it, and the best way to rob other banks is
to own a bigger bank. It might not be possible to
stop this ownership deal, but I might mess it up for
them. Either way, I get a damn good story.

STEFAN
But why on earth were you interested in Tom's
wallet and phone in the first place? What's Tom got
to do with all this?

DON
Absolutely nothing. Pure accident. A mistake.
That was the first story. I thought that Tom had
arranged to meet Maria at the station, and that he was
therefore part of Maria's operation, whatever it is.
So I thought if I found out more about him, I might
get a line on how Maria's outfit operated.

MARIA
Well, Mr. McKenzie, we have now helped you.
You have your text message. Your bank account
number. And a possible scoop. Which I'm sure is
what you are really interested in. But you will *not*
now pursue your original story, is that correct?
In return, I might, just might, decide to give you an
exclusive interview at some future date. If you keep
very quiet now. Is that a deal?

DON
 Yes. I do sort of know what you're up to,
Mrs Kolar. And I do work for the *Guardian*, after all.
We're a good cause too, you know.
And we're losing money very badly—

MARIA
(snorts at this) I think it's time to make our excuses
and leave. I'll call that nice policeman on the way
out. And the best of luck explaining all this to him.

DON
Thank God he didn't find my fake police ID.

TOM
Maria, if we're going, I have some friends who
would rather like to meet you. Just around the
corner—are you free now?

They leave. Don suddenly realises:

DON
Christ, I still need a phone! *(shouts)* Nurse!

Enter Police Officer. He is holding an ID card.

POLICE OFFICER
Now, about this false police ID card
you had on you, Mr McKenzie—

37. INT. IN FLAT ABOVE SHOP. MID MORNING.
BRIGHT SUNLIGHT.

*Roisin & Andriy, Stefan & Maria, and Tom are sitting at the
kitchen table with mugs of coffee. Maria is looking very thoughtful.*

STEFAN
So, if the mafia now have wind of who the
members are, we may need to disband—the end of
the League of Alchemists?

TOM
Which perhaps makes Roisin and Andriy's
suggestions even more useful now.

ANDRIY
Tom has told us the broad outlines, Maria, and we
knew of course about your dot com bubble fortune.
It made some sense. But—

ROISIN
—But we do need to know the *full* story, Maria.
We're not just talking about a small fee per
transaction, are we. But illegal money, yes?
I'm not sure quite how illegal, but my guess is that
you siphoned off an extra *percentage* of each
transaction's actual *value*. Flat rate fees are
predictable. An accumulating percentage can
become astronomical—

MARIA
Yes, you're quite right, Roisin. But it was partly a
genuine accident. We originally wrote the program
to work with currency exchange rates to six decimal
points, the usual inter-bank market convention.
But we also experimented with working to eight
decimal points, just in case. Both worked fine,
and the difference for each transaction was very
small indeed, often less than the exchange rate
fluctuation during the transaction itself. But we also
did the maths and over time the differences in the
overall sums involved became pretty significant.
But our first major clients said they were quite
content with 6 decimal points, so we went with that.
However, the first version of the software we
shipped still had the alternative 8 point calculation
left in. So we just wrote a line or two of code to
bracket out that extra calculation. Then one of our
programmers thought he'd be smart—as a side-
challenge he worked out he could simply *add* the
difference in percentage to our automatic flat fee
account—and do so without alerting anyone who
just checked the 6 point figures. That little
experiment was supposed to be left out of the
upgrade. But you know how it is. Version 0.2
shipped with that wrinkle still there.
A mistake. It happens.

ROISIN
So in effect you had installed a private Tobin Tax?

MARIA
Exactly. And I assure you we didn't realise we had
done so until I spotted it in an upgrade to Version
3.6. By then, of course, we had an interesting
ethical problem. For a start, did we really want to go
to jail? And could we actually recall all the installed
and perfectly working software, and explain why, to
hundreds of blue-chip customers? My husband and
I finally decided to leave it as is, with the hope and
expectation that it could soon be adapted to the
Tobin Tax itself, when that was finally introduced.
All the talk then was that the Tobin would be in
place pretty soon. So we waited to offer an
appropriate 'upgrade'. That was over a decade ago.

ANDRIY
Which means that part of your income was and is
now illegal, and you have the same problem as the
mafia—how to transform illegal into legal cash.

TOM
Or how to make cash from cocaine look like cash
from tobacco. Both deadly in the end.

MARIA
It was worse than that. By now there was so much
accumulated income that if we just left it in the
Swiss account, the Basel Bank would have to invest
it to get maximum returns for the bank to pay us
our accumulating interest, and the sums were soon
so large that it would be difficult to realise a return
without highly speculative and risky investments.

STEFAN
In our own small way, we had become like the
Chinese flooding of the financial markets—

the Chinese economy, that last bastion of state
socialist capitalism, was generating such huge
profits, balance of payments surpluses, and overseas
earnings, that they bought up large parts of the
American economy, including half of US
government bonds —which was part of the
problem with the sub-prime market in 2008—
there was so much Chinese cash sloshing around in
the US banking system that it had to be lent out to
less and less credit-worthy recipients, at riskier and
riskier return rates—and those loans then had to be
covered by ever more risky insurance, by credit
default swaps, and the rest. We weren't on the scale
of China, obviously, but unless we did something
the constant compound curve of accumulation
would make us about the scale of Canada at least!

MARIA
That's when we decided just to give the money
away. And set up the League of Alchemists.

STEFAN
Which we may have to disband now. And find
some other solution. Because the problem hasn't
gone away.

ROISIN
As I understand it, the main point of the League
was twofold: to democratise decisions as to what
donations to make, and to act as cover or blind.
But you can decide on donations in a different way.
Let software do it for you. Simply randomise the
decision—a kind of random lottery amongst charity
and advocacy organisations, a wheel of fortune.
The only decision you have to make is which
organisations are included in the first place.
After that, both the sum and the recipient can be
randomised, a matter of chance, of luck if you like.

It's probably just as rational as asking lots of dying
people to dither over their own bequest priorities.
And a lottery doesn't have favourites or children,
just statistics, betting odds.

ANDRIY
And there's even a simpler way to make the actual
donations as well. You don't want to be traced,
and end up in jail for having the money to begin
with. Well, the normal problem about making
untraceable transactions, stealing money from an
on-line account, for example, is to hack into the
account in order to take the money out in the first
place, and then to conceal where the money went *to*.
Digital theft means erasing the trace of the
destination, the thief who will benefit. But in your
case you want to erase the trace of the *source*, so that
the recipient doesn't know what the source was,
where the money came *from*—and nor does anyone
else. There's no problem about getting into your
account, of course—you control it—you have the
money and a legit account—so all we need to do is
modify the transaction instruction itself, so that it
erases itself and its origin from the transfer trail,
after the actual completion of the transfer, once the
transfer has fully cleared into the recipient's
account.

TOM
I remember William Gibson once wrote a short
story about his dead father which erased itself as
you read it—

ANDRIY
I reckon I can write a pretty simple trojan which
piggy-backs onto the transaction instruction,
 and will erase its own track from the recipient's
records. Most digital theft software is developed

to erase the *withdrawal* traces, to conceal who *stole* the money—so the main security consideration is to prevent the money being taken *out*. But if the issue is to conceal the *donor*, putting money *in*, then bank security is not very alert to that. As for the destination account, all you need is the open public accounts of charities into which the general public can make on-line donations, the websites where you can make a payment by direct trwansfer into a bank account. The magical appearance of several millions from an unknown and untraceable source may be a headache for the accountancy firm involved in doing the charity's accounts, but they can't give the money back — since there's no known donor.

MARIA
I'm an old fashioned lass. I prefer actual people to automated call centres. But I like your ideas so far.

ROISIN
But there is a more radical issue and problem—which Tom was on about last night, and which we can't crack. Yet. How to change the very system that generates the problem, and especially this massive but dangerous sloshing surplus. Can we, or you, buy up and simply *destroy* the assets of the enemy—those of the Koch brothers, for example. Take their money *out* of the system. Like buying a Rembrandt and then burning it. But if you buy, say, Fox News and close it down, Murdoch would just use the money from the sale to set up Rat News. The money stays in the system and accumulates again. Or could we manipulate specific transactions so that the Koch brothers buy some assets at a vastly inflated price—like buying a fake Picasso—and their value then simply disappears. Like the value of Emperor Rudolf's sacred nails. But that probably means, literally, wiping billions off the stock exchange—which is an easy phrase—but is that what we should even try to do?

Won't far too many ordinary people on pensions
and low incomes get hurt as well.

            TOM
Let me just look at your phone, Stefan. *(he opens the
transferred text message).* Just a thought. Here we have
the bank account details of one Viktor Mafia-
whoever. Which apparently has enough temporary
assets in it at the moment to buy a sizeable Swiss
bank. On behalf of some very dubious people I
am happy to think of as the enemy. Can we make
their assets just disappear? Wipe out all those digital
ones and zeroes without sending the money
somewhere else? And also make it impossible for
them to reclaim the money, from back-up records
of the transaction, for example. *(pause)* Perhaps not.
But we can maybe do something pretty close.
A kind of reverse bankers' bonus. We can send it to
the tax man. In fact, to several taxmen in several
countries. I suspect if that happened Viktor's
friends might find it a little difficult to explain quite
why they should have it back—and where they got
it from in the first place. Any thoughts, Andriy?

            ANDRIY
That sounds fun! —let me see. Viktor's account is at
the same bank as Maria's, and presumably the same
kind of premium account as Maria's, and we know
he was there the day before yesterday. The ironic
thing is that banks hold very little physical cash, and
quite probably the actual Euros Maria took out were
those that Viktor had just put in! So, we have his
account number and some useful details. We need
his passcode. Is there a pattern to this bank's
security codes, Maria —does your passcode have to
fit a certain set of rules — number of letters,
sequence of numbers etc., like a computer
password?

MARIA
Yes indeed. It was very strictly specified.

ANDRIY
So his would probably be a variation on yours?
That might not be too difficult. So, all I'll need is a
few tax revenue accounts to transfer his money into!
But this time they need to know *exactly* where these
transfers came *from*. Yes, I shall have fun with this!

STEFAN
Could be very interesting! Most European
governments are imposing hideous austerity cuts to
pay off the 2008 banking crisis 'deficits'. But they
won't impose tax increases on, or stop tax evasion
by, the very wealthy. At least if the tax revenue
suddenly goes up by several billions, it'll be that
much harder to justify the need for 'cuts'. So can
we extend this beyond Mr Viktor? To tax evaders?

TOM
Only if we had access to lots of dubious bank
account details!

MARIA
Well, I could perhaps buy a Swiss bank, or two—

STEFAN *(raises mug of coffee)*
I'll drink to that!

39. INT. VIKTOR'S HOTEL ROOM

Viktor is on the phone and very angry.

VIKTOR
What do you mean—I can't use my account to buy
it. It's legal. I've had it checked out. I warn you—
and it's *my* money! So what's the problem—*(longish
pause)*— what do mean, it's empty! ——what!!

39. INT. MARIA'S HOUSE. LIBRARY.

Roisin and Andriy, Stefan and Maria, and Tom.
Tom has his luggage with him. Wine glasses.

MARIA *(proposing a toast)*
Before I take Tom to the station, let me just say
how glad I am to have found some new friends.
As you know, I have no children of my own,
though I have adopted several orphanages over the
years. And now that the League of Alchemists
seems to be over, and you, Roisin and Andriy, have
left me with very little to do apart from run a
software lottery or two, I will have to find
something new to fill my time. So perhaps I can
partly adopt you, or at least co-opt you—

STEFAN
—You could just relax and take it easy, Maria!

MARIA
Not at all! So I am setting up a new organisation,
called The World IS DEAF—World Institute for
the Study of Digital Economy Alternative Futures.
DEAF for short. And I'd like you all to be part of it.
To do as much, or as little, as you can. The real job
is just to *think through* what kind of alternative
futures *might* be possible. Not to predict, or to
calculate. Not to peer into a crystal ball. But
certainly to hope. Franz Kafka said : "Is there
hope? Yes, plenty of hope. But not for us."
I want to change that last phrase, at least. There is
no magic bullet. But we can begin. To hope.

They drink the toast.

ROISIN
Can I add something, Maria. Before Tom goes, let
me just point something out to him. He remains the
old sceptical marxist materialist, of course.

He does not believe in occult hidden powers, shaping our destinies. He even distrusts our Tarot packs. But look again, Tom. Here we have the benign High Priestess, Maria, secretly shaping many destinies. There is also the Evil Emperor, Viktor, and *his* secretive powers. Don McKenzie was, of course, the Hanged Man, or nearly so. Andriy and I are obviously the Lovers in the pack. That leaves you as The Hermit in your study, as ever—

    STEFAN *(interrupts)*
—So who is the Fool, or Magician?—not me, I hope!

    ROISIN
No, Stefan—the Fool. or Magician, in this Tarot pack, is whoever wrote this script!

40. EXT. AT THE CORNER OF VŠERDOHVA AND RIČNI STREETS. AFTERNOON.

Maria's car pulls over.
Maria and Tom get out and stand in front of the church on the corner.

    MARIA
I hope you don't mind this little detour on the way to the station, Tom. But this is one of my favourite places in Prague. I had the church restored in memory of my dear husband. It was one of the first things I did after he died. *(pause)* It gives me some consolation. You tell me the news from your doctor is bad. And you say you have no faith, no religion. But if there is anything I can do—

    TOM
Thank you, Maria. I do appreciate what you are saying. *(pause, then chuckles)*. I once had to set an exam question on a course entitled 'Religion and Politics'. I suggested:

' "The last thing a marxist wants to do on his
deathbed is to read *Das Kapital*." Discuss.' Well,
you've changed me just a tiny bit, Maria. Perhaps I
shall read that day's *Financial Times* instead. *(smiles)*
What is the church called?

                    MARIA
Svatý Jan Křtitel Na prádle.

                    TOM
Meaning?

                    MARIA
The Church of Saint John of the Laundry.

They both laugh.

41. INT. HOSPITAL ROOM.

Tom is clearly very ill, in bed with many tubes, and very weak.
He is asleep. In his hands is a copy of the Financial Times.
The camera focuses on a minor but front page headline:

   Tobin Tax Software Contract Awarded to Kolar Inc.

CREDIT(S)

                    <u>The End?</u>